Wuthering Heights

Adapted by
Mary Sebag-Montefiore

Illustrated by Alan Marks

Edited by Susanna Davidson
Series editor: Lesley Sims
Designed by Michelle Lawrence
Reading consultant: Alison Kelly
Roehampton University

First published in 2010 by Usborne Publishing Ltd.,
Usborne House, 83-85 Saffron Hill, London
EC1N 8RT, England.
www.usborne.com

Contents

Wuthering Heights family tree

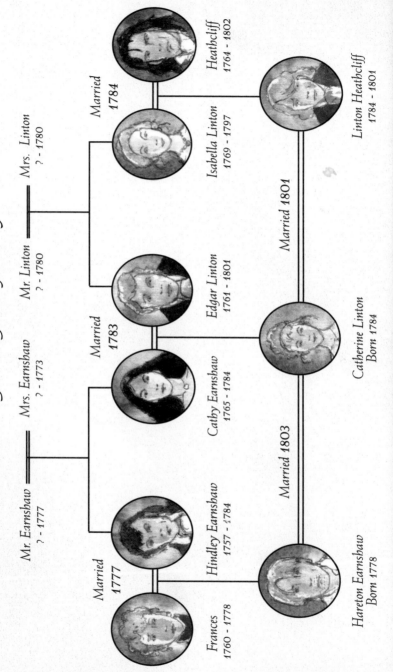

Mr. Earnshaw
? - 1777

Mrs. Earnshaw
? - 1773

Married
1777

Frances
1760 - 1778

Hindley Earnshaw
1757 - 1784

Cathy Earnshaw
1765 - 1784

Mr. Linton
? - 1780

Mrs. Linton
? - 1780

Married
1783

Edgar Linton
1761 - 1801

Married
1784

Isabella Linton
1769 - 1797

Heathcliff
1764 - 1802

Married 1803

Married 1801

Hareton Earnshaw
Born 1778

Catherine Linton
Born 1784

Linton Heathcliff
1784 - 1801

Chapter 1

Catherine's ghost

Mr. Lockwood's diary

The Yorkshire moors that surround my new home and my new landlord, Mr. Heathcliff, are equally described in three words: savage, bleak, brutal. Yet Heathcliff has an air of pride in him, swaggering like a fine gentleman, though his wild, dark eyes and swarthy skin are surely those of a gypsy.

I'm curious. He hides a secret, I'm certain – something blacker than most people experience in a whole lifetime. *What could have made him like this?*

I walked from my house, Thrushcross Grange, to his, Wuthering Heights. It was a long way over the moors, but I was keen to greet my new landlord. Innocent fool that I was! Heathcliff belongs not to the civilized world but to the untamed rocks and hills that surround our homes, where cold winds blow in vicious gusts.

"Come in, Mr. Lockwood," he muttered, in a tone that suggested he meant, *Get out and good riddance.*

There were some fir trees at the front, stunted by the continual wind. The wall bore an ancient date, 1500. One step brought me into a hall, gloomy in the half-light of a dying fire.

It threw flickering shadows on an oak dresser, stacked with rows of pewter jugs. Above it, guns and pistols hung on hooks. Under it, a huge dog growled, surrounded by her mewling puppies.

The mother dog, her lip curled back, pawed my leg. I stroked her... she snarled.

"Don't, Lockwood," Heathcliff sneered. "She's not a pet."

I saw a woman sitting in a chair. Heathcliff's wife, I wondered? As my eyes grew accustomed to the gloom I saw that her young face was the most exquisite I'd ever seen, with golden ringlets on her delicate neck. She looked at me with a strange expression: half scorn, half desperation.

A young man came into the room. I thought at first he was a servant, because he was poorly dressed, with rough, dirty hands. His bearing, though, was haughty.

"Are ye makin' tea?" he demanded.

"Is he to have any?" the girl asked Heathcliff, indicating me.

"Get it ready," was the answer, uttered so savagely that I jumped.

I drank it, thankful for its warmth. I saw snow beginning to swirl at the window panes, thickening steadily in its mesmerizing onslaught.

"This charming young lady is your daughter?" I said.

He shot the girl a look of hatred. "Charming? Ha! She's my daughter-in-law."

"And this young man is your son?"

"He is not. Her husband is dead."

"My name is Hareton Earnshaw," scowled the boy. "Respect it."

"I've shown no disrespect," I replied, feeling uncomfortable. Outside, I saw night settling early, the sky and hills obscured in a bitter whirl of suffocating snow. "I really think," I said reluctantly, "I must ask for a bed here tonight. The roads will be buried; I won't find my way back."

"You can't stay here," Heathcliff said.

"Lend me your lantern, then." As I seized it, eager to leave, his dog leaped at my throat. I fell, bleeding, but Heathcliff merely laughed, saying I'd given him no choice, and called Hareton to show me to a bedroom upstairs.

I set my candle on some mildewed books. Its flame lit names scratched on the wall: *Catherine Earnshaw*, and *Catherine Heathcliff*, and then, *Catherine Linton*.

I picked up one of the volumes. *Catherine's Book* it said on the front. I flicked through its pages, scrawled in a childish scribble, like a diary.

I hate Hindley. He is horrible to Heathcliff. He won't let him sit or eat with us. He blames our father for adopting a vagabond, then he kisses his wife, that silly Frances. Heathcliff and I are planning revenge . . .

Uninterested in playtimes of long ago, I got into bed, blew out the candle and fell asleep.

Tap! Tap! Howling winds woke me, or, yes, I was sure, one of the fir boughs banging at the window made this insistent noise. Tap! And again...

I must stop it, I thought, rising from my bed to open the window.

I pushed my arm out to grab the tiresome branch... Instead my fingers closed on the fingers of a little ice-cold hand. I drew back my arm, but the hand clung to it and a voice sobbed, "Let me in!"

"Who are you?"

"Cathy..." wailed the voice. "I lost my way on the moor. I'm come home. I've been wandering for twenty years..."

Mad with fear, shaking off the fiend's grip, shutting it out, I yelled with all the force of my lungs, "GO AWAY!"

My yell woke Heathcliff.

"What are you doing?" he demanded.

"That g-ghost at the window," I stuttered, "...wicked soul... told me she'd walked the earth for twenty years, a punishment for her evil, I've no doubt."

He pushed me aside, wrenched open the window, bursting into uncontrollable tears. "Come in," he sobbed. "Cathy, do come. Oh do – once more. Oh darling, hear me this time!"

I was terrified. I fled to the hall and spent the rest of the night there. As soon as light dawned, I struggled through the snow drifts over the moor to home.

My cold walk made me ill. A fever kept me in bed, feeble at first, then bored.

"Talk to me," I begged my housekeeper, Nelly Dean, who'd nursed me devotedly. "Do you know Heathcliff of Wuthering Heights?"

She nodded. "I do, Mr. Lockwood."

"Why is his house so gloomy? Isn't he rich enough to keep it up?"

"Rich! He's got money pouring out of his coffers... he's greedy for wealth – strange, when he's alone in the world."

"I thought he had a son?"

"He died, not long after he married young Catherine."

"Where did she come from?"

"This very house, Thrushcross Grange. Her name was Catherine Linton. I was housekeeper to her mother and father, and nurse to Catherine."

"Who is Hareton Earnshaw?"

"Young Catherine's cousin."

"And Heathcliff? Why is he so..." Words failed me.

"I know what you mean," said Nelly Dean. "He's a rough character, hard as granite. Don't meddle with him. You want to know why he's like that? I'll tell you his story..."

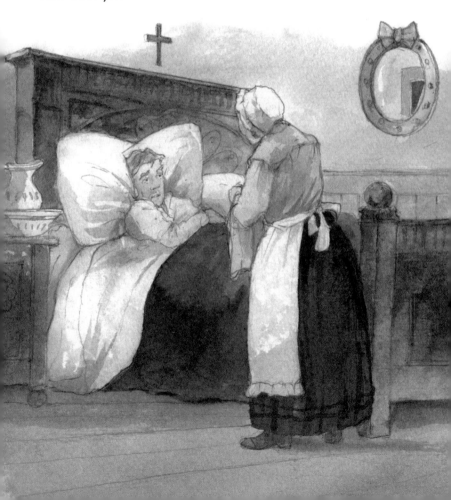

Chapter 2

Wild children

Nelly Dean's Story
Part One

"Before I came here to Thrushcross Grange," Nelly began, "I was always at Wuthering Heights, running errands, haymaking and looking after the children, Hindley and Catherine Earnshaw. One morning their father said, 'Now children, I'm going to Liverpool today. What presents would you like me to bring back?'

'A violin,' begged Hindley.

'A whip for my horse,' Cathy ordered.

Mr. Earnshaw promised, but when he returned, the fiddle and whip in his great coat pockets were crushed by the child in his lap – a dirty, ragged, black-haired brat.

Even though Hindley was a boy of fourteen, he cried to see his fiddle crushed. The child looked the same age as Cathy, but it stared without saying a word as Mr. Earnshaw explained he had found it starving and homeless on the streets.

'Wash it, Nelly,' he said. 'Find it clean clothes, and let it play with the children.'

They called the child Heathcliff, as both first name and surname. Cathy made friends quickly, but Hindley hated him, because Mr. Earnshaw preferred and made a fuss of Heathcliff. Once, Mr. Earnshaw bought each boy a horse. Heathcliff took the handsomest and when it fell lame he made Hindley give up his.

'If you don't,' he threatened, 'I'll tell your father you hit me. He'll whip you.'

'Take the wretched horse,' Hindley spluttered. 'I'll pray it breaks your neck.'

Heathcliff seemed unmoved. He never showed emotion. He was sullen and proud but I still didn't realize how vindictive he could be, as you will see.

Cathy was a mischievous child, high-spirited, her tongue always singing and laughing. She could be naughty, bold and saucy, but she had the sweetest smile and meant no real harm.

Old Mr. Earnshaw died. Hindley went

away and came back with a young wife,
Frances. He made Heathcliff stop his
lessons, work in the fields, and eat alone
in the back kitchen. Heathcliff didn't
mind because Cathy taught him what she
learned. And when they could escape,
they ran off together, to spend the days on
the moors.

They used to laugh at their
punishments; however much Hindley
thrashed Heathcliff, it was forgotten the
minute they were together again. They
grew more daredevil every day.

One day Heathcliff returned alone.
'Where's Cathy?' I demanded.

'Captured, Nelly, by Thrushcross
Grange. We went to spy on those silly
little children, Edgar and Isabella Linton.
We howled like banshees and made them
cry. We dropped off the window ledge
when we heard their parents come; the
fools set their dogs at us, and one caught
Cathy's leg. Then they recognized Cathy,
sent me, the wicked boy, packing, and
they're keeping her until her leg heals. I
watched through the window... they dried
and combed her beautiful long hair, they
washed her feet, gave her slippers, fed her
cake, wheeled her to the fire, and there
she stays, happy as anything.'

Weeks later, Cathy returned,
accompanied by Edgar and Isabella.
She'd become a young lady, very dignified,
with hands white from being indoors and
doing nothing.

'Heathcliff?' she said at once.

Heathcliff was filthy from working in the fields. Cathy drew her dress back from him, exclaiming, 'You look so odd... so dirty.'

'I shall be as dirty as I please,' he stormed, running off.

I followed him. 'Wash yourself; show her how fine you are.'

'I'm not fair with blue eyes like Edgar.'

'No...' I was brushing his hair. 'You're dark and handsome, if you don't look sulky.'

Hindley and Edgar jeered when he came downstairs.

'He's ridiculous, trying to be a gentleman.'

'His hair's like a colt's mane.'

Heathcliff seized a dish of apple sauce and threw it in Edgar's face. Edgar bawled and Isabella wept, calling for home.

'Stop,' Cathy snapped at them, as Hindley dragged Heathcliff away. 'You're not hurt, either of you.'

She knew what would follow... she winced at the sound of Hindley's whip lashing Heathcliff.

I found Heathcliff later, up in the attics, lost in thought. Cathy was with him, holding his hands.

'I'll pay Hindley back, somehow,' he said.

'No,' I interrupted. 'God may punish, but we must forgive.'

Heathcliff smiled. 'God won't have the pleasure that I will. I don't care how long I wait for my revenge.'

Chapter 3

Heartbroken...

Nelly Dean's Story
Part Two

Five years later, there were changes at Wuthering Heights. Frances and Hindley had a baby, Hareton, and soon after, Frances died. I looked after Hareton, a darling, good little boy. Cathy had grown into a haughty, headstrong girl, the queen of the countryside, though she still played truant with Heathcliff when the mood took her. She saw Edgar and Isabella Linton frequently.

Hindley began to drink too much. Little Hareton was afraid of him. He never knew if he was going to be kissed and squeezed almost to death or flung against the wall.

One night, Cathy came in when I was rocking Hareton on my knee.

'Where's Heathcliff?'

'Working in the stable,' I answered.

'Edgar Linton asked me to marry him, and I said yes. Should I have, Nelly?'

'You've given him your word – you've promised.'

'Yes, but... was it right? He's pleasant to be with, he loves me, he's rich, and I'll be the most important lady in the area. But it feels wrong, Nelly, here, and here!' – striking one hand on her forehead and one on her heart – 'in whichever place the soul lives.'

She went on, 'Do you ever dream strange dreams, Nelly? I dreamed I was in heaven but it didn't seem to be my home and I broke my heart weeping to come back to earth. The angels flung me out, here on the heath, and I woke with joy. I've no more business to marry Edgar than I have to be in heaven. I'd marry Heathcliff tomorrow if Hindley hadn't brought him so low. It would degrade me to marry him now. He'll never know how much I love him though; he's more myself than I am. Whatever our souls are made of, his and mine are the same. Nelly, I am Heathcliff.'

'Oh, Cathy,' I began…

'I know you think I'm selfish, but if I married him, we'd be beggars. I can use Edgar's money to help Heathcliff.'

Before she'd finished, I saw Heathcliff come in… and then disappear. He'd listened until he heard it would degrade her to marry him, and run off. He didn't come back.

Catherine married Edgar and went to live at Thrushcross Grange. I went too, as her maid, though I didn't want to leave my nursling, little Hareton. She made friends with Isabella, and lived an easy life of luxury. She was like a thorn embraced by honeysuckle; Edgar, afraid of her temper, gave in to her every whim.

A few years later, I was in the garden, just as dusk was drawing in, when I heard a voice say, 'Nelly?'

A tall man, handsomely dressed, came up to me. He had black, fiery eyes. I would have known anywhere.

'Heathcliff!'

'Tell Cathy I'm here.'

Cathy was so overjoyed to see him that Edgar muttered, 'Can't you be glad without being absurd, Cathy?'

Edgar wasn't sure how to treat him; he'd last known him as a rough, wild farmboy.

'Where are you staying?' he asked.

'At Wuthering Heights. Hindley
Earnshaw invited me.'

Knowing Heathcliff loathed Hindley, I
wondered what mischief he was planning.

Heathcliff visited us constantly, and
Isabella, pretty, naïve and wilful, began
to flirt with him. Edgar was horrified; he
hated to think of his precious sister close
to this unpredictable man, sprung from
an unknown past.

Isabella complained that Cathy wanted Heathcliff for herself. 'You won't let me be alone with him,' she wailed, petting her canary. 'When we were walking on the moor, you stuck by his side, and told me to wander off...'

She pouted. 'I love Heathcliff more than you've ever loved Edgar.'

'Are you mad?' Cathy replied. 'He's too untamed for you; he's pitiless. I'd rather put your canary outside on a winter's day than recommend you to Heathcliff. He's capable of marrying you for your fortune; don't fall into his trap.'

'Not true...' Isabella sobbed. 'Cathy's so mean, Nelly...'

'Beware,' I said. 'No one knows how Heathcliff got his money, yet honest men don't hide their deeds. Why is he at Wuthering Heights? They say Hindley is worse now, he borrows money from Heathcliff against his land and does nothing but play cards and drink day and night.'

Isabella put her hands over her ears. 'Wicked lies! I won't listen.'

'Isabella loves you,' Cathy told Heathcliff, 'but...'

'Jealous?' he sneered.

'No! Do you like her? I'm certain you don't. Don't marry her.'

'If I thought you wanted me to marry her, I'd cut my throat,' Heathcliff said, turning away from her. 'But I'll amuse myself with her, as you have with Edgar.'

Not long after, Isabella ran away with Heathcliff. Edgar's reaction was as unforgiving as I'd expected.

'She's chosen to cut herself off from us,' he said. 'I never want to see her again.'

Isabella wrote to me...

Dear Nelly,

As Edgar won't answer my letters, I'm writing to you. Wuthering Heights is horrible. Hindley is dirty and drunk. When I asked where my bedroom was, Hindley said, "I don't want you here." When I explained I wanted Heathcliff's bedroom, he drew his pistol. "Lock your door," he said. "If I find it open, neither of you is safe."

"What has Heathcliff done to you?" I demanded, and he replied, "I will have my land back, and my money too."

He's mad, and as for Heathcliff, is he a man or a devil? What have I married? I hate him. Oh Nelly, I'm so unhappy.

Isabella

Chapter 4

Unquiet souls

Nelly Dean's Story
Part Three

After Isabella went, Cathy became very ill. She was heavily pregnant by then, but that wasn't the cause. She was shocked that Heathcliff had left her for Isabella. Edgar was patience itself; you could tell how he loved her, but she seemed so sad.

One Sunday morning when Edgar was in church, Heathcliff came, alone.

'Well, Heathcliff?' she gasped. 'You've broken my heart. You've killed me.'

'You think I don't suffer too?' he blurted.

'Why should I care? I'll die, and you'll forget me. No, I can't bear it...' She held out her arms. 'Come to me.'

He flung himself at her, saying wildly, 'Why did you despise me? Why did you betray your own heart? If you die, how can I live?'

'If I've done wrong, I'm dying for it,' sobbed Cathy.

'Quick,' I said. 'Edgar will return any minute. You must go, Heathcliff.'

That night, Cathy gave birth to a daughter, and died two hours later. The baby is Catherine, the young girl you met at Wuthering Heights, Mr. Lockwood.

I had to tell Heathcliff that Cathy was dead. I found him outside; he'd never left the grounds.

'How did she die?' he asked.

'Quietly,' I said. 'Her life closed in a gentle dream.'

'May she wake in torment,' he cried. 'Catherine Earnshaw, may you never rest. You say I killed you – haunt me then. Be with me always! I can't live without you.'

Her coffin lay uncovered in the drawing room, strewn with flowers. Until she was buried, Edgar stayed there day and night, a sleepless guardian. He didn't know that outside, Heathcliff paced his garden.

Her grave is in the churchyard where the plants climb over the wall from the moor.

A week later, as I was rocking baby Catherine, Isabella burst in.

'I've run the whole way from Wuthering Heights,' she panted. 'I'm leaving that fiend... why did Cathy love him?'

She hurled her wedding ring into the
fire. 'There! Let it burn! Edgar won't help
me. I've come for my clothes and then I'm
going. Heathcliff was so angry, he threw
a knife at me. Oh, Heathcliff's destroyed
me, Nelly, and Hindley too. He's not
human – since Cathy's funeral he hasn't
eaten or slept at home.'

Sorry as I was for her, I longed for news of my little Hareton.

'How is he?' I asked. 'Tell me about him.'

'A detestable child! An animal! If I try to kiss him, he throws a stone at me. I'm having a child too, Nelly. Heathcliff's baby. Heathcliff must never see it!'

Months later, she wrote to me. She'd gone to London and had a baby boy – Linton.

I told Heathcliff of the child, though not where they lived. He was neither pleased nor displeased; he said with a grim smile, 'I'll have it when I want it.'

When that time came, Linton was twelve and Isabella was dead. She'd paid a high price for her impulsiveness.

Chapter 5

Heathcliff's revenge

Nelly Dean's Story
Part Four

During these years Cathy's baby, little Catherine, grew to be a beautiful child, combining the best qualities of her father and mother. She was spirited and gentle, winning and thoughtful. Her love was never fierce; it was deep and tender. Her father, Edgar, adored her and if he had a fault in her upbringing, it was over-protectiveness. During her childhood she never left her garden.

'What lies on the other side of those
hills?' she asked me. 'The sea?'

'No,' I answered. 'Just hills again, like
these.'

'And those golden rocks?'

'Penstone Crags,' I told her. 'They look
gold because of the sunset.'

'I must get there,' she sighed.

When Catherine was thirteen, Edgar received a last letter from his sister.

I'm dying, Isabella wrote. *Please, for my sake, look after my boy, Linton.*

Edgar was glad to make amends, and Catherine was excited to have a cousin.

'He's six months younger than me,' she chattered. 'We'll have such fun together!'

Linton looked very like Isabella, fair and delicate, but there was a sickly air about him, which Isabella never had. Catherine was kind to him, petting him like a baby, and indeed, he behaved like one. He lay on a sofa; he had no energy to run and play.

Soon after Linton's arrival, a messenger came from Wuthering Heights.

'Heathcliff wants his lad,' he said, pointing at Linton. 'I musn't go back without him.'

'Who wants me?' Linton cried, growing pale.

'Your father,' replied Edgar. 'He has first claim on you. You must go to him.'

Linton began to sob. 'I never knew I had a father. I'm frightened, uncle. Let me stay here.'

'All parents love their children,' I said to comfort him, though I was never less sure of anything. 'Don't let him see you're afraid. I'll take you there myself.'

'What's he like, Nelly?' Heathcliff asked as he greeted us – then laughed scornfully. 'What a beauty! Worse than I expected. Have they fed it on sour milk?'

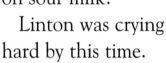

Linton was crying hard by this time.

'Stop,' ordered Heathcliff. 'I won't hurt you. Flaxen curls! Where is my share in you, bony chicken? Hareton, bring him food, then get back to work. Yes, Nelly,' he continued, seeing me astonished, and unhappy, too, that Hareton had forgotten me. 'Hareton is my servant. Hindley is dead; Wuthering Heights is mine. This miserable brat whom I hate for the memories he revives, is my heir.'

'Be kind to him,' I said.

'I've no wish for him to die, Nelly. I'll have the triumph of seeing my child, my property, as lord of the countryside.'

Hareton came back with some porridge.

'Ugh!' exclaimed Linton. 'I won't eat it.'

'Just like his mother, always moaning,' growled Hareton.

I slipped away, but as the latch clicked on the door I heard the boy repeat frantically, 'Don't... Oh, don't leave me...'

Edgar wouldn't let Catherine visit Linton; he didn't want her near Heathcliff. We told her Linton was far away.

On Catherine's sixteenth birthday I took her for a ramble on the moor. Edgar was feeling unwell and wanted to be alone.

Catherine ran in the sunshine, pretty as a wild rose with her hair flying behind her. 'One more hill, Nelly. This way... to golden Penstone Crags...' she called.

'Turn back,' I said. We were getting near Wuthering Heights.

Too late! Heathcliff was striding towards us over the moor.

'Nelly Dean and Catherine! You must be tired,' he said silkily. 'Come to my house... and see your cousin Linton.'

'Who are you?' faltered Catherine.

'Linton's father. Won't you come?'

'Don't, Catherine,' I warned. 'Your father won't like it.'

'Oh, I must, Nelly. Poor Linton! I want to see him.'

She covered Linton with kisses. He looked, I thought, ill and languid.

'Naughty Nelly,' she scolded, 'telling me Linton lived far away. Why couldn't I come here?'

'Because your father hates me,' said Heathcliff. 'He thought I was too poor to marry his sister. If you want to see your cousin again, keep your visits secret.'

I pulled him away, demanding, 'What are you planning, Heathcliff?'

At first he was silent, then he blurted out, 'Nelly, if only Hareton were my son, not Linton. Linton is pathetic, a useless scrap. But I could have loved Hareton, if only he'd been someone else...

I know what Hareton suffers, because it's what I suffered myself. I've kept him so ignorant, he can't even read. He's coarse... low... he lives in dirt – he's just a servant. Oh yes, I'm even with Hindley at last. Look what I've done to his son.'

He gave a fiendish chuckle before declaring, 'And Linton must marry Catherine. That way, I'll be even with Edgar too.'

Catherine crept up to us, pointing at Hareton who had joined us; he looked rough and awkward.

'Who is that?' she asked.

'Your cousin also,' Heathcliff replied.

Catherine, the little minx, whispered something into Heathcliff's ear, which made him laugh.

'She says you're handsome, Hareton,' Heathcliff teased. 'Take her around the farm and try to be interesting. There...' he added, as Hareton blushed scarlet. 'I've tied his tongue. See how gormless he is.'

Back home, Edgar was furious when Catherine confessed where we'd been.

'If it wasn't for Heathcliff, your mother would be alive still. Never go again. That man is evil and you are my beloved girl!' His cough shook his whole frame. I knew he wasn't well.

'But poor Linton.'

'Enough!' thundered Edgar.

And that, I thought, was that, but months later, tidying Catherine's drawers, I found a pile of Linton's letters hidden there.

'How could you disobey your papa, when he's so ill, writing to Linton?' I asked her.

'I love Linton.'

'Love!' I snorted. 'You don't know what it means.'

'He needs me, Nelly. I'm going there, now.' She raced out of the door... I'd never seen her so defiant.

She ran to Wuthering Heights.

I learned later what happened. Linton begged her to marry him. She hesitated, but Linton pleaded. 'Father wants it. He's afraid of my dying if we wait any longer. He won't let you out of the house. The doors are locked.'

'I won't stay! I'll burn down the doors!' she shouted. 'Papa's ill; he'll worry about me – I love him better than you.'

Heathcliff burst upon them. 'Crying again, Linton? You shall stay!' he shouted at Catherine. 'You'll be married tomorrow. Your father will think you've run off for

some amusement... soon he'll be dead, and then I'll be the only father you have!' As she tried to flee, he hit her head, and she fell back, dizzy and powerless.

'You must obey him,' Linton wept.

The next day, as she became Linton's wife, Edgar grew really ill, coughing blood. I knew this meant the end was soon. He murmured constantly, half-conscious, *Where is she? Oh, Catherine darling, come home!*

I couldn't bear him to suffer. I ran over the moor and knocked at Heathcliff's door. To my relief, he was out and Linton answered. 'Have pity,' I begged. 'Please let Catherine say good-bye to her father.'

'Dying, is he?' he muttered. 'Then Thrushcross Grange will be mine. Father says everything that belongs to Catherine is really mine.'

'Let her come,' I insisted, and this time he listened. Catherine, weeping, was able to kiss her father before he died.

55

After Edgar's funeral, Heathcliff refused to let Catherine stay at Thrushcross Grange.

'Why not let her live here, with Linton and me?' I suggested.

'Keep her in luxury? No. She'll work for her bread. I'll get a tenant for the Grange.'

'I'm sorry for you, Heathcliff,' Catherine said. 'Nobody loves you. No one will weep when you die.'

'Quiet,' bellowed Heathcliff, seizing her. 'Go back to Wuthering Heights!'

'Good-bye, Nelly,' whispered Catherine, hugging me. 'Don't forget me.'

...I haven't seen my sweet Catherine for months..."

Chapter 6

Rest in peace

Nelly Dean finished her tale, but I knew the end of the story was yet to unfurl.

"When did Linton die?" I asked her.

"Not long ago." I saw she was weeping. She said, "I keep thinking of my two dear nurslings, Hareton and Catherine, once so loving, and now abandoned. If only they were happy."

"I'm not sure I want to stay at Thrushcross Grange any longer," I said. "The scene of such grief. I'll ride over and tell Heathcliff I'm going."

Heathcliff was out, but I saw Hareton and Catherine who seemed as sad as before.

Yes, I thought, *she's a beauty, but she's so surly and spiritless.*

Suddenly she said, "Mr. Lockwood, will you tell Nelly I can't answer her letters because I haven't any paper or even a pen. Please, ask her to send me some books."

"What books?"

"Anything. Heathcliff destroyed all mine, and I do so want to teach Hareton to read."

"I'll bring them myself," I promised. Now I, too, saw a glimmer of her charm.

When I brought over the books, she and Hareton were laughing together. All his sulkiness had vanished, and his rudeness, while her smile was sweet as honey. I could see a bond between the two of them, more than a spark... an invisible fire that lit their eyes and warmed their joined hands.

"We're going to plant flowers here," she told me. "We'll bring them from Thrushcross Grange. Hareton has pulled up some bushes to make room for them."

At that moment Heathcliff strode into the room. He had overheard her last remark.

"How dare you?" he shouted.

"You shouldn't grudge me a bit of earth when you've taken all my land and money."

"*Your* land and money, insolent girl? It's all *mine*."

"You've stolen Hareton's too. Hareton and I are friends now; you can't frighten us any more."

"Stop staring at me," he shouted. "You look like your mother... Hareton looks like her too. Oh Cathy, Cathy, Cathy..."

I left them. I explained I had no wish to rent his house any more, and rode away.

Six months later, I was in Yorkshire again, and called on Nelly. Heathcliff, she told me, was dead. He'd suddenly stopped eating and drinking, as though he'd willed himself to his grave.

"It was Hareton and Catherine's love for each other that ended his power over them. It sapped his strength. I saw him before he died," she said. "He was strange."

"How?" I queried.

"He talked of Cathy... he saw her everywhere, in every cloud and tree. He said he felt in the shadow of change, that Hareton and Catherine reminded him of himself and his immortal love. *Oh God*, he said, *I wish it was over*."

"The night he died," she went on, "a little shepherd boy on the moor after dark came running, crying, saying he'd seen Heathcliff and a woman walking arm in arm. Who can say who or what he saw..?"

At last she smiled. "Hareton and Catherine are married and living at Thrushcross Grange. The ghosts of the past rest in peace."

I said goodbye to Nelly and walked over the moor. I passed by the church and found three gravestones there. One was old, half buried by heath, Edgar's green with turf, Heathcliff's still bare.

I lingered there, under that calm sky, watching the moths fluttering among the harebells. As I listened to the soft wind breathing through the grass, I wondered how anyone could imagine unquiet slumbers for the sleepers in that quiet earth.

Emily Brontë
1818-1848

Born in Yorkshire to a large family, Emily and her brother and sisters started writing at an early age, creating imaginary lands. Emily published *Wuthering Heights*, her only novel, at the age of 29. People weren't sure what to make of it at first, but it is now one of the most famous books in English literature.

Emily's sisters, Charlotte and Anne, also became famous writers and the Brontës' home at Howarth Parsonage has now been turned into a museum.

Howarth Parsonage, Yorkshire, England